Spanish lesson

* Optional (tambourine, tabor drum or castanets)

* Or a few voices

Ghosts of the past

*Or a few voices.

Dreams of the fu - ture, __ ghosts of the past left be-hind.

doo doo doo doo doo doo doo doo doo doo doo doo doo doo doo doo

doo doo doo doo doo doo doo doo doo doo doo doo doo doo doo doo

ah ah

(ah) __

mp p

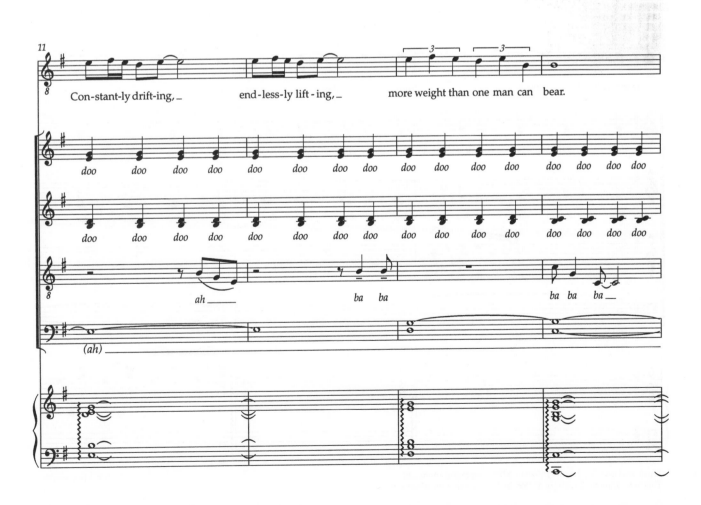

Con-stant-ly drift-ing, __ end-less-ly lift - ing, __ more weight than one man can bear.

doo doo doo doo doo doo doo doo doo doo doo doo doo doo doo doo

doo doo doo doo doo doo doo doo doo doo doo doo doo doo doo doo

ah __ ba ba ba ba ba __

(ah) __

TENOR SOLO

Ghosts __ of the past.

mm _____

mm _____

mm _____ ah ____ doo doo doo doo

mm _____ ah ____ doo doo doo doo

(optional)

Toss-ing and turn-ing, __ some-how I'm learn-ing __ se-crets I'd ra-ther not

doo doo doo doo doo doo doo doo doo doo doo doo

doo doo doo doo doo doo doo doo doo doo doo doo

Working women

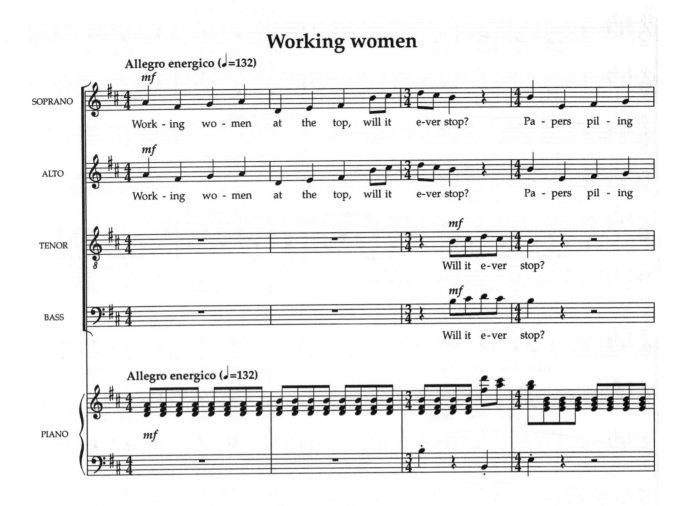

* Or a few voices, or full

* Or a few voices, or full

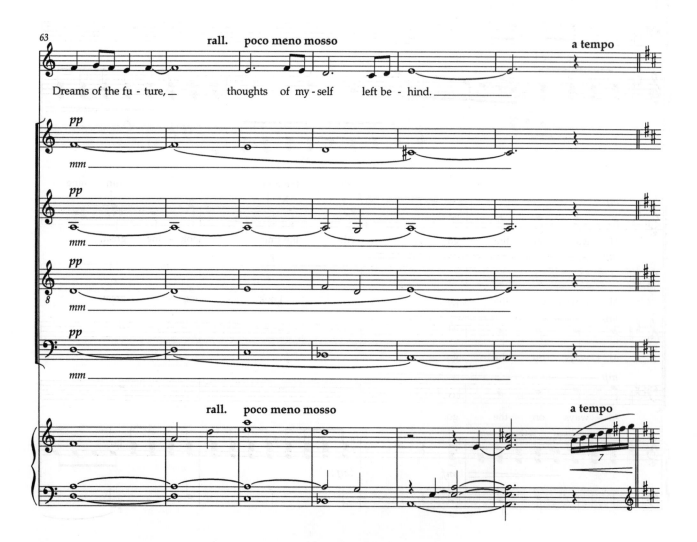

Drinking song

* ⌐ 2nd time only (optional)

you.

If ev - 'ry - bo - dy took a

se - rious view of life, we all would feel the same as you. But, as it is, we don't, so it is - n't gon - na

oo ____

bo - ther us.

Let's have a drink while we think what to

doo ____

I'll ac - cept a lit - tle drink from you.

do. ____ And while we think, I'll ac - cept a lit - tle drink from you.

Save the child

*Or full

* Alternatively, divide Sopranos equally between top two parts.

Family life

Choral Programme Series

For mixed voices:

Benjamin Britten – Christ's Nativity SATB (div)

Anton Bruckner – Six Sacred Choruses SATB/organ or piano

Antonín Dvořák – Four choruses for mixed voices Op 29 SATB

French Chansons – Saint-Saëns/Fauré/Debussy SATB & SATB/piano

Gustav Holst – Five Partsongs Op 12 SATB

Felix Mendelssohn – Four Sacred Partsongs SATB (div)

C.H.H. Parry – Seven Partsongs SATB

Henry Purcell – Five Anthems SATB/keyboard

Franz Schubert – Four Partsongs SATB/keyboard

C.V. Stanford – Seven Partsongs SATB

Ralph Vaughan Williams – Three Choral Hymns SATB/organ or piano

Giuseppe Verdi – Choruses from 'Il Trovatore', 'Nabucco' and 'Aida' SATB (div)/piano

Five English Folksongs (arr. Runswick) SATB

Five American Folksongs (arr. Runswick) SATB

Gilbert & Sullivan – Opera Choruses 1 SATB/keyboard

Gilbert & Sullivan – Opera Choruses 2 SATB/keyboard

A Gospel Christmas – Spirituals for the festive season (arr. Runswick) SATB/piano

Lloyd Webber – Memory and other choruses from 'Cats' SATB/piano

Lloyd Webber – Mr Mistoffelees and other choruses from 'Cats' SATB/piano

McCartney/Davis – Choral selection from Liverpool Oratorio SATB/piano

Schwartz – Gospel choruses from 'Godspell' and 'Children of Eden' SATB/piano

For upper voices:

English Edwardian Partsongs SA/piano & SSA/piano

Fauré & Saint-Saëns – Six Motets SA/organ or piano

Franz Schubert – Three Partsongs SSAA/piano

Robert Schumann – Eight Partsongs SA/piano & SSA/piano

Lloyd Webber – Memory and other choruses from 'Cats' SSA/piano

Lloyd Webber – Mr Mistoffelees and other choruses from 'Cats' SSA/piano

McCartney/Davis – Choral selection from Liverpool Oratorio SSA/Piano

Schwartz – Choruses from 'Godspell' and 'Children of Eden' SSA/piano

ISBN 0-571-51433-2

Faber Music 3 Queen Square London WC1N 3AU

9 780571 514335